www.finishinglinepress.com

Somewhere Like You

poems by

Jennifer Flescher

Finishing Line Press
Georgetown, Kentucky

Somewhere Like You

ACKNOWLEDGMENTS

"Sisyphus and the Ants" was published in *Poetry Magazine*. "Plum Island,
August" was published in *Nixes Mate Review*.

Thank you: Dr. Anna Samoilov, Dr. Daniel Geller, Dr. Jennifer Rathbun
and the late Dr. Harriet Berman. Sage and Blake—I got the best ones. Kim,
Deana and Laura, my first readers. Also the HIY group and especially Peentz
Dubble, with whom the bulk of these poems were written.

Publisher: Leah Maines
Editor: Christen Kincaid
Cover Art: Jennifer S. Flescher
Author Photo: Jennifer S. Flescher
Cover Design: Elizabeth Maines McCleavy

Printed in the USA on acid-free paper.
Order online: www.finishinglinepress.com
             also available on amazon.com

Author inquiries and mail orders:
Finishing Line Press
P. O. Box 1626
Georgetown, Kentucky 40324
U. S. A.

Table of Contents

For Blake

Running Aground

Sometimes the earth reaches
toward you
from a depth or your own
inability to see what's there.

In those times
when space has bent around you
before the movement stops
there is nothing to hold on to

nothing to stop the future
force of impact
the blood inside to out
torn skin.

What you want or try
or how accepting
has no bearing.
Just the rocks through the bottom

of the clear, clear merging,
just the way they promise
to tear away
all that contains.

Maternal

1.

I never wanted to have children. I think I was a teenager when I decided that; years before my mom left the country, more years before I became a mom. There are other decisions I've made in my life that somehow seem counter—counter to culture or counter to heart... cynical decisions. Decisions born of wounds.

I felt that life was mostly painful. I didn't want to be like any of the parents I knew—who mostly seemed selfish and unhappy. But more than that—life was something sharp and brutal. Something not to be inflicted.

Cleanliness

When you won't wash yourself, I
am washed in fear, and the memory of the body

sweet stench of the lobby sleeper on Grant Avenue.
The man who swore quietly

and wore burlap and bare cracked feet
blue and brown and pink.

He whistled like my father, or a nightingale.
Your nails are long and filled with food.

Children are walking across Europe, stranded
and hungry in herds.

Your teacher told me you were beginning to smell.
The children noticed too.

I want to worry myself into your fingers.

If I could live there, sleep
and take my meals, then I could wash you every morning

like when you were first born, and a little blue.

2.

I first remember wanting to die when I was ten. I tried to piece together whether or not I could slit my wrists with a butter knife. It seems sort of sweet now—to look back at myself as that small creature—before breasts, before geometry.

I guess it seemed somehow painless, though I also remember thinking it would take a lot of force. Or maybe it was simply that I wasn't allowed to touch the pointed ones with the black handles.

That day I asked my mother what she would do if I ever killed myself. We were in Maine, in the middle of seventeen acres of poison ivy. She just answered—as if maybe the voice in her head was speaking to her, not her child. She said she would probably kill herself too. That was the end of that. I wasn't looking to murder anyone.

I asked her about that conversation a few years ago. She said it never happened, but I'm pretty sure she saved my life. Or re-inflicted it.

Three Years Before My Son Attempted Suicide

his teacher, Jim, died. Jim wore a red cap and a white beard and spent 37 years teaching kids to read on the stuffed-animal loft in that disheveled room and when I say died I mean he killed himself. In April. When all the six and seven-year-olds were on break, and our boys were at the Boston marathon and it was bombed. There was no shade. My son only asked two questions, after two years every day reading on that loft one on one. One was did he use a gun.

Letter from Barre
—For Jim

The branch brush falls into unity
into a burnt umber haze on the mountain

from this distance, in this earliest spring.
Was your car facing the river? The water

still shallow from freeze, the crown
of the smooth stones holding their places.

Was a robin, in his bold-breasted future, watching?
Did you watch him fade?

Isolated trunks stand, lit by birch peels and the glow
of the going down. Each tree stands so firm

one would not possibly ever argue to another, fallen:
How could you take yourself away from me?

As if it was your right? A bird's nest
never seems precarious as it is—sharp things

softened and curved and holds the children.
And home is gone now. You were the home.

3.

When you look up the word in the condensed OED (a book which by its own physical nature helps me mark time by the need this morning for the long-lost magnifying glass it came with) you have to go pretty far to get past a definition that simply defines maternal as being a mom. Relationship to other. I suppose this is part of what causes a lot of pain for mothers who lose a child: the question of a definition based on one state of being. I was surprised to feel that pang, years after both of my children were born, when I had to have a hysterectomy. I felt strangely severed from some sense of womanhood; some sense of purpose. You have to go down nearly to the end of the definitions to move into where society obsesses: having the instincts of motherhood; having the ability to provide the requirements of motherhood.

Years before my children were born, their father announced, at a social gathering, that he thought I was the least maternal person he knew. I felt wounded. What is a woman supposed to be more than maternal? And anyway, I love to feed and soothe people. It wasn't until years later—or maybe this morning—it occurred to me maternal is only a word subject, like all language, to an individual life. When my son was born I told his father's mother I was completely in love with him. She said "that's good. That isn't always the case for mothers with their sons."

I love being a mother. I feel like it is the one thing in the world, however much I screw up or struggle, that I truly understand.

And mostly, for me, I think it was biology. I was an animal, driven like the tide, and no intellectual, spiritual or psychological layerings could change my course.

Whale Requiem

She was lying on her side perfectly still
as if the only thing out of place
was the location of the water
and the air. As if they had changed
places overnight.

*

We came upon her, entering another world.
Baleen and her mouth open, gently.

Everyone said, *that's so sad.*
They flocked to the scene, the news
the Facebook walls. Gawked, *Tragedy.*
Was it her size that makes them
make that noise with their eyes?
The black and white?

I wash up every day. Fall ashore
from where I am meant to breathe.

*

Sympathies were aborted a few months later
when a great white shark
bared teeth just down the coast.

It's a warning.

People only mourn
if you go quietly, don't threaten
to take anything down with you
or show your hunger.

*

They yellow taped the scene
before beginning
the whale autopsy. Students came with green boots,

knives and saws.
They peeled back the skin. Disassembled the body.
Huge hunks of fat piled in black plastic Hefty bags.

Ribs one by one into the back of a silver Ford pick-up truck.
The man with the green stocking hat and hook held one up for me
to take a picture—the length of his whole torso.

Then waved it at my dog. *Want this?*

*

Want this? What kind of an idiot, I thought
but the dog didn't bite. She looked scared.
Maybe she could smell the dying fish
calling for the deep and distance.

When they pulled the intestines out like coiled
industrial vacuum pipes I thought about my own
hysterectomy. How they laid my insides outside.
How after I was bruised and empty.

*

And then it was gone.
I thought some realms should be impenetrable.

That, and what can live and die can disappear.

The scientists and students took away the carcass,
the water took every trace of blood.

From one day to the next anything might have never been.

4.

After my psychotic break I was shattered. At the time, I called it a nervous breakdown, which sounded softer to me.

I still haven't experienced anything that has hurt as much as going on Lithium. At the time, I thought the pain was part of the break, but after watching my son begin taking Lithium I became convinced that it was the medicine. All I can say is that it felt like someone was taking a chisel to my head—then pounding it with a hammer. As my head was splitting in two all I could hear was the metal on metal crashing over and over.

I could no longer trust my mind. I can only recall that sensation vaguely now. Like trying to remember being in love. Those emotions that absorb every moment of life and your perception of how everything works together as a whole. I suppose I took reality for granted before—and maybe I do again. Knowing that you can look out of your eyes and see some representation of a horizon that at least off-handedly resembles the representation your neighbors' eyes perceive. I didn't hallucinate or hear voices, but I did think the news was sending me messages. I did think I was part of some giant experiment that had me at McLean Hospital, observed and charted like a rat. Sometimes I would make rat noises, to try to explain to my friends and family, or to try to explain to the people watching behind the cameras on the ceiling, I knew what was real.

Plum Island, August

On Plum Island the sand descends
as if the world ends
and the sea takes on the hue of deep
close to the shore.

We drifted in the calm
built a castle
found fractured purple mussel shells.

You had just come home, hollowed.
If we slept at all it was huddled
in nightmares.
You'd grown tall and small at once.

You made friends with a girl half your age
and the two of you played
with the breath of the sea.
I watched you almost laugh.

You said you wanted to go there
to make me feel better. I had that feeling
on the raft of that day.

Library of Footprints
  [a stolen poem]

What does the ocean want with our footprints? he said.
We were walking where the dry sand and waves

take each other in. Watching the trace, watching the wash away.
What does it do with them?

His voice was still high. He hadn't grown the foot he would that year.
Maybe the ocean keeps them all, he said.

He was just home from the hospital.
Somewhere locked away.

A student told me, on any given day,
40,000 teenagers attempt to die.

Maybe it has us all catalogued and numbered.
Maybe it has them all in a giant library of footprints.

Then he said, *That's my poem, Mom. You can't have it.*

5.

It was like being taken under by the ocean. The cold force drags you—then you have sand in your mouth and you are watching the sky distance itself from you. Direction makes no sense and you are immobile and crashing simultaneously. Maybe blood greets the sand and you know that it is entirely possible you will not live because the power of Mother Nature has asserted itself.

When you are on the beach, and have finally expelled all the salt and water from your lungs and the tears from your eyes, you know for the first time
death is always that close.

I felt betrayed by my own mind and body.

I suppose that is when I decided to have children. I wanted a house. I wanted two kids. I wanted to forget that I had ever thought I knew something better about how to swim, light and thinking, through the world. I wanted to disappear into normal.

6.

I have always been very careful. I suppose that is also to say I have always been afraid, but I don't know if I ever thought of the two as connected; except in the sense that I was always jealous of women who didn't worry about everything all the time.

I went off Lithium eight months before trying to get pregnant, under the supervision of my psychiatrist who is still one of the smartest most thoughtful women I have ever known. She was my only psychiatrist, but having known many now, she is still the best I've seen.

I went to the high-risk pregnancy unit at Mass General Hospital in Boston. I knew that psychosis could sometimes reoccur in childbirth. Careful.

Somewhere Like You

I could hear the fat cooking
from the neighbor's grill.

The lawn was brown in spots and the herbs
were competing with weeds for air.

The tree was covered—
those huge white flowers that dwarf the yard

and make the tree feel
like it belongs somewhere else.

Like it deserved a better life.
Somewhere like you.

7.

I remember the waiting room was big and cold, even though it was filled with women with huge bellies and strollers and pacifiers. I remember blue and gray and light-colored wood. I don't remember the doctor, or the room I went to, even though I would visit those rooms again many times. I do remember what he told me.

We recommend that you do not have children. That is what he said. I was highly likely to pass on my illness through maternal genetics. The odds were exponentially higher than average my child would commit suicide.

It felt like sterilization. Like engineering genetics—or even humanity. I reminded my psychiatrist of this conversation years later, when I took my son to her. *I remember when they said that to you,* she said. *I was so mad—that was so wrong.* She told me that at the time, too. She said not to listen. I'm not sure how much of an impact that first conversation had, but if it had any it would have been to go forward with it all, if only as a political condemnation of the hospital's position.

I wonder a little now, though, if they weren't just saying the same thing I had been saying for years before.

Life is so incredibly hard. More so when you want to die every day. Why would you ever inflict that on somebody else.

May You Be Without

"an evil done or sustained" (OED; definition of "harm.")

By

Brick
Fingernails
Teeth
A bully of a seven-year-old boy
A doctor
A father
Thumbtack
Medication
The contents of a stress ball, ingested
Sarcasm
Medication again
The volume of rap music
Light socket
A garden stake
A roommate
One's own mind
Temperament
An administrator
A father, again
A grandmother
Garden stake, again
Memory
Impulse
Bottle of hard cider
Nails, again
A basin of water
Champagne
An ocean
A pillow.

8.

That one three-week stay in the psychiatric hospital was my only exposure to the mental health system as a patient. I became obsessed with the media for a while—the violent and damaging depictions of the mentally ill. We were like sharks after Jaws... But after Lithium I was more stable than I had ever been. And that stayed. Knock on wood.

My son has had a harder road. He is only 15, but over the last four years he has been in seven programs, with two hospital stays, six psychiatrists and a dozen medications. Aside from the pain his own biology and experience has brought him, he has been misdiagnosed, overmedicated, medically ignored and injured, within some of the best settings in the country. I list these afflictions only to say that the system is a tsunami in and of itself. If his own mind drags him to the bottom of the ocean, the mental health system has been a boat, coming to stop above him and block out the sun and the direct path to air, even as it looks like only way to land. If you are unlucky the boat has propellers.

My son is a brilliant light. He teaches me about being human every day. He makes me a better person through his incredible perseverance, strength and creativity.

Despite all the indignation I feel towards that doctor at MGH, it is still his voice I hear when I am most afraid for my son's future. On some days, the fact that I am never sorry for an instant that I had him makes me wonder if I am unbearably selfish.

Sisyphus and the Ants
—after Jack Gilbert

The story tells us Sisyphus is being punished.
Over and over he has to push that boulder

up and up. The mountain and God glaring.
And you, you have

your avalanche of moods.
Pills the size of stars to nearly quell

cascade and tumult.
And still you step

gravity amplified by incline, each hazard
in the way of the boulder a reminder

it should be easier. There should be
a hot fudge sundae at the top. A long nap in the shade.

The story forgot to tell us, though, Sisyphus thrived.

He learned to guide his wrists
and shoulder girdles safely to protect himself.

And later he worked to safeguard every insect
from here to the crest. Considers this his calling.

Even as the sun and the weight of time bears down.
Your strength is kingly.

9.

What I am learning most is detachment. I have been studying yoga philosophy deeply over the last several years, and it helps me move through this time.

Last summer in study group we were discussing detachment and desire. People talk about every day desires. About wanting material things. Or wanting a book deal or a husband...

My teacher said, she struggled with it too. That she wanted to help her students. That she wanted to be able to give them what they needed.

The girl with the dying mother said, there are good wants and bad wants.

That's not right, though.

I wanted my son to be well. That is a good want. I would not want to want otherwise.

But the fact remained he was not well. And my spending any time at all wanting him to be well was taking me out of the moment I was in, and my ability to see clearly and focus on the time at hand.

I am trying to make sense out of all of this, I suppose.

But maybe this isn't anything any different from the seascape every other mother has to confront. In high school a friend beseeched for understanding, how could she possibly have children when they could get hit by a car walking across the street.

Maybe that's all maternity is—accepting the lack of control linked so completely to the biological and species-oriented drive of responsibility for the carrying on. It is our job to help them survive it all and the ocean.

Maybe the only difference is that I was warned.

How to Make it through The Night

Sometimes the body—this whole world—
comes with an overwhelming wall of speed and strength

tides turn tsunami and can't be endured.
Sometimes this happens

in the mind. My daughter is afraid of vomit.
She wasn't feeling well or wasn't feeling well about not feeling well.

It's hard to tell from the shore.
Eventually she drifted into my bed. Eventually I slept.

Do you know how I made it through the night? she asked.
How easily we, dry, forget the feel of frigid blue lips. The deep tremor

of near frozen. *I prayed for every single person*
I could think of. And then myself.

J **ennifer S. Flescher's** poetry has been published in publications including *Poetry, The Harvard Review, Lit, The Boston Globe,* the blog for Best American Poetry and numerous anthologies. Her non-fiction about poetry has been published in publications including *Agni-online, The Harvard Review, Poetry Daily* and *The Boston Globe.*

She holds an MFA in Poetry from Lesley University and an MsJ in Writing and Reporting from the Medill School of Journalism at Northwestern University.

For ten years she edited and published *Tuesday; An Art Project,* an unbound, letterpress printed journal of poetry, photographs and prints.

She currently lives with two teenagers and two German Shepherds. She teaches writing and yoga in Newton, Massachusetts.